Accents on Accessories

IDEAS AND INSPIRATIONS FROM SOUTHERN ACCENTS

Library of Congress Catalog Number: 95-79007
ISBN: 0-8487-1452-0
Manufactured in the United States of America
First Printing

Accents on Accessories

Southern Accents₀
Editorial Director: Katherine Pearson
Editor: Karen Phillips Irons
Managing Editor: Lynn Carter
Art Director: Ann McKeand Carothers
Copy Chief: Tami Arnold
Production Coordinator: Candace H. Schlosser
Editor-at-Large: Philip Morris
Features Editor: Lydia Longshore
Entertaining and Travel Editor: Karen M. Carroll
Art and Antiques Editor: Frances M. MacDougall
Southeast/Southwest Editor: Elizabeth S. Betts
Art Assistant: Lelia Catherine Still
Copy Editors: Jeanne Destin, Elizabeth Emery White
Copy/Production Assistant: Maria Parker
Office Manager: Carol Walker
Editorial Assistant: Lydia DeGaris
Stylist: Ashley S. Wyatt

Oxmoor House, Inc.
Editor-in-Chief: Nancy Fitzpatrick Wyatt
Senior Homes Editor: Mary Kay Culpepper
Senior Editor, Editorial Services: Olivia Kindig Wells
Art Director: James Boone
Editor: Brenda Waldron Kolb
Designer: Seunghee Suhr
Editorial Assistant: Laura A. Fredericks
Assistant Art Director: Cynthia R. Cooper
Copy Editor: Susan Cheatham
Copy Assistant: Jennifer K. Mathews
Production and Distribution Director: Phillip Lee
Production Manager: Gail H. Morris
Associate Production Manager: Theresa L. Beste
Production Assistant: Marianne Jordan
Senior Production Designer: Larry Hunter
Publishing Systems Administrator: Rick Tucker

Jacket: styled by Dan Carithers, Atlanta;
photographed by Charles Walton IV

Cover: fabric "Briton" by Rose Cumming Chintzes, Ltd.,
through Ainsworth-Noah, Atlanta;
photographed by Charles Walton IV

CONTENTS

INTRODUCTION

Chapter I

A PORTFOLIO OF APPROACHES

What accessories can accomplish for you

Chapter II

ESSENTIAL ELEMENTS

A short course in effective display

Chapter III

PERFECT PLACEMENTS

What works best, room by room

Chapter IV

IN SEASON

Fresh approaches to seasonal decorations

Chapter V

YOUR OWN STAMP

Accessorizing to express yourself

INDEX
CONTRIBUTORS

THE NEW HAVEN CLOCK CO. NEW HAVEN

de of the Dresden, with its unusual Georgian Revival stone window
one of the most handsome in Washington.

west corner. The residents of
have opened the wall to
to create a spect
two drawing roo

The fifty-su
build in 1909. In
in 1910. In 1910
American Securit
Benjamin H. Ward
changed from rental to

Since the Dresden's property, includ
he rear, it was possible to conve
lot for eighteen cars, a rare
apartment house. During

Many of the conversion to co
and stayed when
These included Mrs. Nellie Tayl
woman governor (Wyoming, 192
rector of the United States Min
the administrations of Frankli
S. Truman. Others included M
social secretary to Mrs. Rich
and Mrs. George H. Millhol
the former Alice Wardman
and original owner of the Dr

Another interesting to
at the Dresden is Helen
grandfather, Jean Pierre S
ington from Paris by Pre
to become the first manag
of the White House. Wit
Dolley Madison save th

$500,000
000 to
amount to the
trustees of the
remained rela-
At that time Wash

S T O R Y T E L L I N G is really what accessories are about—stories about family, heritage, interests, quirks. For instance, the vignette at left, which is in the home of Washington, D.C., designer Joe Davis, tells us a great deal about him. His fascination with his city's history is literally an open book; a page depicts his apartment building as it looked decades earlier. A French doré clock is a clue that, like many collectors, he has a keen appreciation for the decorative arts of other times and places. Native American pottery speaks of connections west of the Potomac. ● I N D I V I D U A L I T Y like this has never been so highly prized in accessorizing. Think back to the predictable decorating of the 1950s, when we bought furniture in suites and accessories to match the furniture. Because furnishings followed a prescribed formula, those interiors now seem to us lifeless and unimaginative. At the opposite end of the scale are the highly personal homes we're drawn

I n t r o d u c t i o n

to today—homes whose artworks and decorative objects reveal the history and character of their owners. ● F O R Y O U R F A M I L Y S T O R Y, you should create an environment with a narrative thread that's distinctly your own. The accessories you choose should reflect your point of view and lead to an apt conclusion. Success depends not only on the individual pieces you select but also on how you display them. And that's where this book—with its inspiring photographs, practical ideas, and well-seasoned advice— can help. ● W E ' L L S H O W Y O U H O W some of the South's best designers and confident homeowners have assembled collections and displayed them to advantage. Seeing exactly what they've done to give their favorite objects pride of place—on tabletops, mantels, shelves, and walls—will give you lots of ideas to try in your home. And since individuality is the goal, you'll find these strategies realized in many different styles and scales, making it easier to relate them to your own personal style and story.

CHAPTER I

WITH INSTINCTIVE FLAIR, Atlanta designer Dan Carithers had only to pull together pieces his client already owned to make this tabletop compelling. For many interior designers, such artful ease is second nature, but it's a skill that you can learn. In the next few pages, we examine the work of Carithers and three of his well-known colleagues. Close inspection reveals a few guidelines that you can follow in a variety of settings. ● DECORATING BY ROTE is definitely not the route. Instead, these designers follow a simple rule of thumb: Focus on what's special to you. Incurable collectors all, they believe you can't go wrong when you favor what's meaningful over what's merely popular. Whether it's pillows or paintings, if you choose pieces that strike a chord within you, somehow they'll work together

A Portfolio of Approaches

in your home. ● THE NEXT STEP is to arrange things to look their best. Despite their distinctive styles, the four designers featured here use the same fundamental techniques, which we elaborate on in this chapter. To call attention to favorite objects, they may use neutral backgrounds or special lighting. To make a collection of disparate pieces come together in a single composition, they may organize them in a symmetrical arrangement or group them according to color. Accenting differences, on the other hand, is sometimes a means of making their point. ● A CONFIDENT SENSE OF STYLE is all about knowing which approach best suits you. These four designers show that your individual style will emerge when you begin with highlighting what's important to you.

*D*AN CARITHERS

A c c e s s o r i e s, believes Carithers, are the most important ingredient in making a room come alive. "More than any other element," he says, "they reflect your personality, calling to mind stories about a particular vacation, a person you admire, or an interest you've pursued." What defines your style, though, is not just the character of the pieces you select, but how you live with them. In this client's sitting room, Carithers nonchalantly leans a Matisse print against book-filled shelves. Nearby, he fills a fine porcelain vase with tulips. Though the vase is museum-caliber, Carithers confidently pulls it into everyday use. "What makes owning something extraordinary even more wonderful," he reasons, "is getting to enjoy it every day."

"**Neutral hues** are the most accommodating," says Carithers. "A soft, natural palette has endless potential and can change with your collectibles or even the season. Add some blue-and-white porcelain, and suddenly you have a blue room. Set out a few bouquets of pink tulips in the spring, and you have a pink room."

"Collections," says Carithers, "are like old loves and new loves. The combination of the two is forever changing, and that allows your interiors to evolve." For instance, this Palm Beach dining room was almost complete before Carithers installed a pair of antique French tapestries. They provide a framework for the room's other elements, which can be rearranged as mood strikes or occasion requires.

ᏀERRIE BREMERMANN

Balance and proportion distinguish Gerrie Bremermann's style. In her New Orleans home, the designer exhibits both virtues in the classical organization of pairs of tole candelabra and architectural ornaments placed on either side of a beautifully carved mantel. Decidedly French in her approach, Bremermann often adapts the continental salon—a large room divided into several small seating groups—to Southern settings. In one client's dining room, she introduced a fabric-covered round table and banquette in a corner opposite a rectangular Art Deco table and bamboo opera chairs. The client approves, saying that the cozy corner is perfect for entertaining a few friends, while larger groups of guests are relieved of having to sit at one long, boring table.

"Symmetry unifies eclectic accessories," says Bremermann. Here, family coats of arms, French memorabilia, and antique tole pieces provide the frame. Whether she adds or subtracts smaller pieces on the tabletop, the entire composition will still seem complete.

"**C a s u a l   e a s e** comes, ironically, when you pay attention to detail," observes Bremermann, and her coffee table is a small but effective example. Instead of placing the flowers in the center, she pulls them to one corner so they share importance with other elements on the table.

MARY DOUGLAS DRYSDALE

The last layer of detail in a home's design scheme includes the accessories, believes Mary Douglas Drysdale, a Washington, D.C., designer. "They polish a room," she says. When she adds these final elements to an interior, she relies on a classical organization of colors and shapes to create formal balance and pleasing proportions. Nothing is left to accident. A subtle instance of this is seen in the foyer of a home where she arrayed black-accented pillows on a settee to repeat the black in the rug's stenciled pattern. Despite the thoughtful order that underlies Drysdale's designs, she works at keeping her rooms from being too serious. A free spirit at play, she collects gilded ceramic fruit and groups them on a tabletop for a surprisingly informal addition.

Contrast is a hallmark of Drysdale's interiors. In her living room, a rough-textured statue by Manuel Neri stands between fine silk draperies. Nearby, a colorful ceramic sphere is juxtaposed with a neoclassical-style table.

Expected with Sam Gilliam's three-dimensional painting might be Barcelona chairs in chrome and leather, but Drysdale substitutes antique George III chairs. She adds one more surprise to the room: Frank Gehry's corrugated-cardboard armchair, a functional work of art.

"**A r t** is essential to any decorating plan," Drysdale says. "Paintings and sculpture fill voids in our rooms and in our lives, while adding drama and energy to our environment." Compelling sculptures such as a smaller version of *Gloria Victus* by Mercié give visual weight to the tabletops.

LEXANDER BAER

Chiaroscuro, the careful manipulation of light, character-izes interiors by Alexander Baer. The library of his Baltimore home is a masterful example of how lighting can act as an intangible accessory—evoking mood, enhancing function, and calling attention to special objects. First, he wrapped the room in a soothing dark color. Then he installed small portrait lights to draw the eye to the fine art on the walls. An opaque shade on a desktop lamp focuses light on the table's surface, while translucent lampshades by the sofa create a softer, more diffuse illumination for the entire room. To follow Baer's lead, create inviting pools of light in dark-walled rooms such as libraries, dining rooms, and bedrooms—areas most frequently used in the evenings.

P a t i n a, which comes only with age, is a quality Baer prizes. Over a table in his library hangs an eighteenth-century portrait of a French noblewoman, a striking counterpoint to a Robert Motherwell serigraph over the sofa. Baer's fondness for fine old things isn't limited to his paintings and porcelains. Whenever he moves to a new address, he also takes with him his eighty-year-old damask draperies.

H o s p i t a l i t y and amusement go hand in hand in Baer's home. In the guest room, he complements a bowl of potpourri with loose dried blossoms placed on a flower-painted tabletop. Bilston and Battersea boxes offer guests a peek at the designer's porcelain passion.

T w e l v e of everything—that's Baer's rule for collecting porcelain plates. He rarely bothers to coordinate his purchases with his dining room colors. His approach is simple and applies to most any collectible: "My greatest love is china. If it appeals to me, I know it'll work in."

CHAPTER II

HAVE YOU EVER WONDERED why some rooms work and others don't? What distinguishes the two isn't necessarily a matter of style. A room patterned after the English country mode—with an abundance of prints, pillows, pictures, and overstuffed furniture—may feel more ordered than a cleanly furnished but haphazardly organized contemporary space. Skillful accessorizing can make the difference, and knowing how to evaluate the results is the key. ● AN ADAPTABLE FRAMEWORK does indeed exist. Despite the vagaries of fashion, some simple guidelines for effective display are evident in every beautifully designed room. Balance, interest, emphasis, rhythm, unity, and scale are constants. They inform the choices that designers make every day. In practice, though, these rules are so sensible that they are

Essential Elements

really just a distillation of common sense. ● TRICKS OF THE TRADE work best when they naturally evolve from your particular situation. In the example here, the late Joe McKinnon, respected Birmingham designer, raised the mirror to fit more comfortably in his high-ceilinged room. To fill in the resulting gap, he hung a framed leather piece below. A pair of tole branches brackets the arrangement and gives it balance. Together these pieces create an effective background for the bust, but it's the jolt of blue from the glass bowl that mitigates the formal setting and draws the eye. ● SUCH FLOURISHES are part of a designer's stock-in-trade. No hard-and-fast rules exist, of course, but understanding the basics lets you know when to observe and when to push the limits. This chapter is a short course in those very basics.

ORMAL BALANCE

Pairs prevail: If there's one on the left, there should be one on the right. Simply put, that's the principle behind formal balance. Among the oldest of design precepts, it was a basic tenet of Greek and Roman architecture, and it endures still in many Southern settings. In the foyer of this home, for instance, Atlanta designer Nancy Braithwaite pairs columns and urns to emphasize the balance we associate with such classical elements as fanlights and barrel-vaulted ceilings.

Matching chairs, both fine examples of Baltimore painted furniture, bracket a table with the same pedigree in the entry hall of antiques dealer Stiles Colwill's Maryland home. Artworks on either side of the mirror have the appearance of balance though they don't match. On the floor, a basket of old caps leavens the seriousness of the antiques.

P e r f e c t l y matched lamps and vases are symmetrically arranged on a French Empire commode in designer Stephen Black's Baton Rouge living room. The repetition of pairs promotes a feeling of stateliness. Such strict organizations are best suited to a home's formal areas. **N e o c l a s s i c a l** style, in its current revival, highlights sets of furniture and decorative objects. Black observes this kind of quiet order throughout his living room, where the fireplace provides an axis for the pairing off of chairs, artwork, and accessories.

Informal Balance

Today we value comfort and casual style more than ever before. The trend is reflected in an easygoing way with accessories and art. It also accounts for the appeal of informal balance—the appearance of balance achieved with objects that don't necessarily match. Atlanta art dealer Duncan Connelly and his wife, Cris, make the concept work by breaking up pairs of candlesticks. They instinctively add an antique mercury glass ball, which both draws the eye and helps to give visual heft to the lone candlestick on the right.

Wire obelisks (garden topiary forms) and unmatched side chairs lighten the rhythm in the Charleston living room of designer Amelia Handegan. She begins with a formally balanced arrangement and then introduces one or two eccentric pieces to ease the formality.

Candelabra made during the Arts and Crafts period create a satisfying stability for a 1928 painting by Alfred Maurer. On their own, these three pieces would constitute a handsome mantel arrangement, albeit a rather formal one. The inclusion of Albert André's study of Renoir is serendipitous, for the smaller work invites you to step closer to examine both paintings. With the pair of napping porcelain cats, the vignette signals that—no matter how fine the pieces— this home is not a museum. Often it's nonchalant, even playful, counterpoints like these that attract and intrigue.

I
NTEREST

Plate stands, table-top easels, wood or marble cubes, and other low supports are some of the tools for effective display. Best if unobtrusive in both form and color, they allow you to manipulate heights and create visual interest for any grouping. With his Limoges china, Atlanta architect Henri Jova uses dark bases and plate stands to present the pieces with their best faces forward.

A quartet of Ming dynasty figures, when they're placed on platforms of different shapes and sizes, achieves a pleasing variety of heights. The collection brings to mind another guideline that many designers swear by: Always group objects in odd numbers. Here, the Chinese figures are joined by a single bas-relief plaque of similar style, a simple addition that prevents what would be a static foursome.

Books create a platform for a box and porcelain poodles in a well-orchestrated tablescape by Oklahoma designer Francie Faudree. Smaller pieces in particular benefit from being displayed on a modest base, which might be of leather, wood, marble, or any other material that doesn't distract from the accessory itself.

A Staffordshire lamp rises on a small stack of books so it can illuminate an appealing tabletop display. Atlanta designer Jackye Lanham alluded to the home's mountain setting by incorporating rustic materials and deer motifs in porcelain and leather.

A palm towers over a compelling still life in an interior designed by New York designer Vicente Wolf. The tabletop can be viewed from all angles in the central hall of Ruth and Michael Burke's Natchez home. In bringing together some of their favorite things, they relied on a few helpful principles—such as using odd numbers and varying heights and shapes—to compose a vignette that's both pleasing and personal.

E MPHASIS

White on white—the pale palette dramatizes four primitive figures in Dallas designer Jan Barboglio Feldman-Macdonald's serene living room. While a large collection is most effective when massed, a few special pieces will make a bigger impression if you isolate them for impact. Even the shelf disappears into the background.

A broken egg, deliberately placed, draws attention to a beautiful mantel in a home designed by Mary Douglas Drysdale. Because many of us look without seeing, we need some sort of visual surprise to focus our gaze. In this classical context, for instance, we expect accessories such as a Grecian-style urn and an architectural watercolor, so we don't really take note of them. It's the cracked ceramic egg that catches the eye and helps us appreciate the other fine elements.

RHYTHM

Repetition of form is a fashionable way to enrich your decor in an orderly manner. The technique often comes into play on the mantel, as on this corbeled mantel designed by Montgomery architect Jim Barganier. A successful lineup requires at least three pieces and usually more, depending on the size of the items and the width of the mantel. In any case, aim for an uneven number, and arrange them close together so they read as a procession.

Spanish candlesticks all in a row anchor the dinner table of designer Joe Davis. Together with a sweeping line of lilies-of-the-valley, they bring to the occasion a ceremonial grace. Davis's example is useful: Filling different vases with the same readily available flower is an appealing alternative to an expensive, and expected, floral centerpiece.

Antique frames are popular—as well as versatile—collectibles. In the entry hall of Amelia Handegan's home, two large gilded ones (both flea-market finds) help to create rhythm. The empty frames also solve a problem of scale: Without them, the paintings they surround would be too small to hold their own in the spacious hallway.

Subtle repetition has its own harmony, as designer John Chrestia finds in his New Orleans home. A French barometer, with a round face and moving hands, reiterates the features of a bronze doré clock.

$\mathcal{U}$NITY

C o l o r, even in small doses, is a great unifier, pulling together disparate elements and making a room feel complete. In this light-washed room of primarily neutral hues, the soft violet fabric covering a chair and ottoman is particularly welcoming. Across the room, an arrangement of purple irises on a table introduces a deeper hue of the same color, connecting the two areas within the larger space designed by Montgomery architect Robert F. McAlpine.

C o h e s i o n in a grouping is easier to achieve if you repeat the same color in three or more objects. The strokes needn't be broad, either. For the tabletop here, rust is the common denominator. The rich tones of an antique frame echo those of a lamp behind, and the russet color appears again in the decorative band on a crackle-glaze vase.

CALE

Good design has everything to do with pleasing proportions, and accessories can change visual scale for the better. Designers such as Nancy Braithwaite know that it's not enough to arrange a tabletop; the space beneath a leggy table needs to be considered as well. Here, bedside matters are greatly improved with a small book bench nestled underneath a Biedermeier table. The bench serves two functions: It fills in the empty space, and it holds a convenient stash of bedtime reading materials.

Sculpture underscores the symmetrical organization of accessories in Howard Adams's West Virginia home. A Grecian bust anchoring the space beneath the table repeats a theme begun with prints of classical Greek figures and a Wedgwood basalt tea set.

A b o v e a chest or armoire, there often appears an awkward expanse even more noticeable in a room with a high ceiling. Charlotte designer Cindy Smith visually heightens her late-seventeenth-century English cabinet with an urn and platter, both of an appropriately substantial scale.

Bookshelves over a banquette must be high enough to clear the head of someone seated below. But the resulting blank space beneath the shelves can seem unfinished. In an artful solution, Atlanta designer Candler Lloyd lined up antique prints to fill the void.

CHAPTER III

THE OLD ORDER had a place for everything: a sofa and matching side chairs for the living room accessorized with brass candlesticks and a ginger jar lamp. Today we're in the process of rethinking decorating rules we once took for granted. For one thing, we've changed the ways we use the formal living room and other rooms such as the kitchen and master bed and bath. These changing functions of conventional rooms are based on a practical pattern of everyday use of the space, and, likewise, older and more formal rules of accessorizing are giving way to more individual approaches. ● OPPORTUNITIES for fresh design and personal significance have never been greater. The focal point of the living room is almost always the fireplace. Think of accessorizing the mantel and the space above as a chance to set the style of the entire

Perfect Placements

room. Above the fireplace in the Kentucky home of Ben and Jean Matthews, an antique portrait is unframed, suggesting we not take this gentleman too seriously. Exuberant bouquets and wooden rabbits are further signals to relax guests even among fine pieces. ● CREATIVE LICENSE is compelling in other rooms, too. In the dining room, table matters have greater flair—a trend that embraces not just the centerpiece but all of a setting's elements. Appropriate accessories for bed and bath are more broadly defined: Table lamps and antique storage pieces can make the bath as sophisticated as any other room. We're accepting that the kitchen is where guests are inevitably going to congregate, so we're introducing more personality there as well. ● LEADING THE WAY are designers who apply these new perspectives with skill and imagination. In this chapter, we explore their ideas for accessorizing within the larger context of a full room.

ℒ IVING ROOMS

Traditional furnishings such as these seem new when Dan Carithers gives conventional touches a little twist. Centered amid a grouping of compatible (but not matching) chairs, a tieback-wrapped ottoman provides an element of surprise. Airy swags complement the French doors for an effect that's formal without being stuffy. A mixture of stripes, plaids, and florals in coordinating fabrics makes for a successful decorating formula. Here, in soft pastel hues, they soften the formality of the room while opening up possibilities for accessories in a wide range of colors.

Perfect Placements

Texture animates subdued color schemes—a precept ably applied in an Atlanta living room designed by Nancy Braithwaite. Silk draperies, woven grass shades, quilted upholstery, and a sisal rug are highly textured surfaces which create visual interest usually generated with color. Rich wood tones add depth to the light furnishings.

Large spaces, particularly those with high ceilings, call for large-scale artwork, but a set of related works is a viable alternative. With less than an inch of space between frames, this quartet of European prints coalesces into a single composition.

Perfect Placements

For clients who are active patrons of the arts, Washington, D.C., designer Thomas Pheasant uses their traditional accessories in a sparing, uncluttered style which reflects his own contemporary approach to design. Placed off-center, a vase of white tulips and a porcelain bowl simply dress a round table.

E n h a n c e a room's architecture, and then engage accessories that reflect the client—that's Pheasant's strategy. He creates a focal point at the far end of this expansive living room with a wall of well-organized bookshelves that frame a niche, where he displays a painting by Lani Irwin. Drawing on the power of repetition, he positions a bronze sculpture to echo the form of the grand piano.

DINING ROOMS

A loosely arranged floral design by Lyman Ratcliffe is complemented by decorative spheres which extend the centerpiece right up to the place settings. The technique eliminates the jarring effect of an isolated centerpiece floating by itself on a sea of wood. Spirited touches of blue in the sheer ribbons, service plates, and monogrammed place mats spark the monochromatic color scheme.

Round tables are popular for a reason. They offer seating that's congenial and effortlessly equitable. In a setting designed by Robert F. McAlpine, just a few accoutrements dress the table for a formal occasion: half a dozen unmatched candlesticks, a silver caddy mounded with soft green moss, and a simple bouquet of full-blown tulips.

Perfect Placements

A sideboard in Ben and Jean Matthews's
dining room is paired, not with the expected mirror or
painting, but with an overhanging bookshelf showcasing porcelains. The collection brings individuality to a
room that is too often furnished in an uninspired way.
Staffordshire figurines parade along a table in a linear centerpiece. Plain white pitchers and
mugs mix congenially with the porcelains, each holding
a single kind of flower, adding height to the grouping.

Furnish a dining room as you would any other room of the house and create new possibilities. An upholstered love seat tucked in a corner provides pattern and warmth in a room of hard surfaces. A tea table makes this a cozy spot for afternoon sherry.

Overhang the mantel with pieces appropriate for the table and underscore the unusual amenity of a fireplace in a dining room. In the Coke-Garrett house, where Colonial Williamsburg's president lives, Dan Carithers accessorizes the space with pitchers, platters, and plates.

Antique jeweled bracelets are called into service as napkin rings with panache. The bracelets are part of a collection of antique jewelry, which the host, a jeweler himself, enjoys bringing out and allowing his guests to use and admire at a formal dinner.

C o m b i n i n g different china and crystal patterns and different candlesticks on the same table creates a setting with a singularly dramatic sense of style. To unify the table, Mary Douglas Drysdale advises assembling pieces of the same color and degree of formality.

Green glass in three shades enlivens traditional silver and dark wood. "I never set a table the same way twice," says host Stiles Colwill. Fortunately, the fashion for mixing patterns allows you to collect pieces over time and use several on one elegant table.

Formal dining no longer requires starched linens. Place mats are acceptable even for dressy occasions, especially if you own an antique table with a rich patina. The cozy effect of the fireplace and circa 1740 beams is enhanced by numerous personal objects.

Bedrooms

S t y l e can be supremely sensible when you rethink old formulas for private spaces. Architect Robert F. McAlpine treated this master suite with the same design sophistication used in the rest of the house. In the bath, for instance, the marble vanity is mounted at a comfortable seating height. The sink, instead of being recessed, rests on the vanity at standard height, with fixtures incorporated in the mirror above. Treating the sink as a decorative accessory and introducing flattering table lamps make for a bath that is both less conventional and more appealing. In the bedroom, McAlpine appropriated the feeling of a more public part of the house with a hexagonal table that acts as a hub to connect all the other furniture in the room. Considerations like these make the master suite a retreat worth coming home to.

L i g h t and airy conditions abound in Sherry Durlach's farmhouse near Charleston. In her bedroom, Austrian shades allow sunlight to stream in during the day while providing privacy at night. A Venetian mirror hung in front of the window acts like a chandelier crystal, refracting and reflecting light in all directions. By comparison, the spare, straight lines of contemporary lamps seem clean and restful.

S u i t a b l e in hue and scale, a Chinese garden stool acts as a small table between a chaise and chair. Palm Beach designers Mimi McMakin and Brooke Huttig created the corner in a room made peaceful with a palette of blue and white the undisputed favorite among color schemes for the bedroom.

Dark walls wrap a room in warmth. In his bedroom, designer Alexander Baer painted walls a deep cocoa; lush bed hangings of batiste and brocade deepen a sense of sanctuary. The intimacy of a bedroom invites art and accessories with special meaning. Here, Baer can savor his favorites: over the mantel, a Modigliani drawing; over the demilune table, a Henry Moore study; and hanging over the bed, a Renaissance portrait painted on a wood panel.

Dressing rooms, especially if they're artfully arranged, exude calm and composure, becoming an orderly oasis in an otherwise crowded day. Silver brushes and bibelots collected over the years are arrayed on a bamboo table. With rich woods, a bronze bust, and decorative wall sconces, Baer creates a dressing room as refined as a gentleman's library.

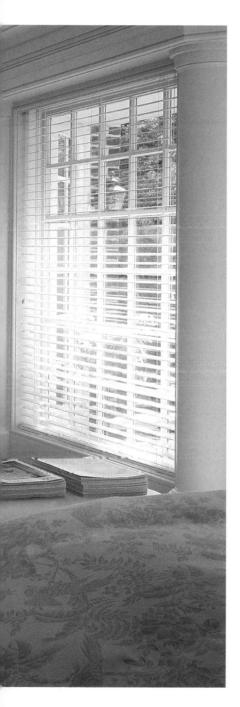

Large strokes, together with small touches, make this remodeled bedroom immensely liveable. Finely crafted millwork was added by Thomas Pheasant to make eight-and-a-half-foot ceilings seem more substantial and to lend stature to furnishings below. Neutral fabrics serve two ends: They provide tranquility and play up the dark wood of fine antiques. **Tabletop topiaries** echo the shapes of the round mirror and a sphere of dried poppy pods and set up a subtle repetition that is always a successful element in great style.

Perfect Placements

Gather harmonious pieces for an elegantly low-key dressing table. Accessories such as wooden tea caddies, leather boxes, and lamps with marbleized paper shades flatter the golden tones of a tiger-maple chest. The lamps establish a balanced framework for a collection of boxes and brushes owned by designer J. R. Miller of Middleburg, Virginia, and Washington, D.C.

Old-fashioned warmth is conveyed in this bedroom by blanketing it with compatible patterns. Extending the scheme established by floral wallpaper and draperies, Birmingham designer Jane Hawkins Hoke fashioned a garden of painted, printed, and fresh flowers.

Balanced pairs of candlestick lamps and bronze vases filled with flowers provide a structured background for the usual dressing-table clutter. When Jackye Lanham adds rustic accents to the feminine setting, symmetry escapes predictability.

Furniture is a great choice for a bath off the bedroom precisely because it's unexpected. New Orleans designer Patrick Dunne uses a freestanding steel-and-glass rack to hold towels and toiletries. A nineteenth-century French curule seat is another notable addition.

Twin beds dictate a formal balance, but in this Tulsa guest-room, designers Dale Gillman and Francie Faudree stave off stuffiness with a bold mix. Flea-market quilts mingle with cheery gingham and stripe-and-floral chintz for colorful, comfortable charm.

*K*ITCHENS

Blue-and-white porcelains are arranged on a kitchen counter and wall by Austin designer Gay Ratliff, just as they might be on a chest in the sitting room or on a sideboard in the dining room.

A chandelier and classical architectural detailing are cues that this working kitchen is as worthy of guests as the living room—illustrating the recent trend toward decorating the kitchen with more individuality. As architect Robert F. McAlpine says, "Everybody always ends up in the kitchen anyway, so you'd better make it look good."

An upholstered settee and unmatched chairs replace typical breakfast-room furniture in the Houston home of antiques dealer Brian Stringer and his wife, Kathi. Collected objects and plush pillows contribute to an atmosphere that's warm and inviting.

Plate collectors will appreciate Stringer's methods for maximizing display: hanging Palissy ware on a wall, displaying dinnerware in a rack, and standing platters at the back of a counter. The shiny surfaces contrast with the more natural ones of green herbal topiaries.

Forgo the formulaic—and think of the kitchen as simply a well-furnished room. In his own kitchen, Alexander Baer incorporates non-culinary accessories, such as a decorative table lamp and artwork, with the essential appliances of a gourmet kitchen.

French country fabrics and wallpaper are currently popular for the kitchen, combining the sophistication of Gallic design with the informality of rural origins. The table can be made larger with a plywood circle disguised beneath a floor-length cloth.

E x p a n s i v e tables call for generous center-pieces, which can be costly. For Brian and Kathi Stringer, a grouping of French pottery provides ample scale filled with wildflowers and cuttings from the garden. Apples heaped in a large container achieve a scale appropriate to the imposing pewter collection behind.

W h i t e —clean, crisp, and light—is always a good choice for the kitchen, but it can seem too cool. Atlanta designer Kathy Guyton warms this large space with old wood pieces and wicker furnishings. An antique plate rack breaks the line of glass-fronted cabinets, and a small table serves as a work island.

CHAPTER IV

LIKE GREAT CHEFS who build their menus around fresh produce that's available locally, today's most inspired floral designers work with whatever their region and the season offers. No longer content with fashioning tight knots of flowers shipped in from hothouses, designers now favor loose, casual bouquets that look as though they had been picked from a nearby garden. ● IMAGINATIVE arrangements today often use flowers judiciously or not at all. Soft green mosses, rangy twigs, wild grasses, rough-textured seedpods—these are only a few of the materials being used to suggest nature's subtle beauty. We're learning to look at natural materials in a new way. As these floral designers are teaching us, even stones from the yard can become part of an evocative display. ● THE CASUAL EASE of seasonal

In Season

accessorizing is enticingly represented here in Mary Jane Ryburn's loosely bunched flowers. Deep blue-purple flowers offset the mottled green glaze of an antique Austrian vase. Alabaster fruits underscore the cool, effortless beauty of the grouping. ● THE NATURAL APPROACH also extends to containers. Gorgeous vases will always have their place, but these days professionals feel free to anchor their displays in wicker baskets, antique porcelains, aluminum pails, recycled glass bottles, or wooden fruit crates. It's all part of the trend away from the studied and toward the unaffected. ● THIS NEW DIRECTION is fortunate for those of us who like to have in our homes some small reflection of the changing season. Now it's both less expensive and much easier to accomplish.

*S*PRING

Leafy vases, such as these cornucopias, are so interesting that you needn't spend a lot on flowers to achieve a grand effect. Marcel Wolterinck, a respected floral designer from Holland, created these horns of plenty for the Royal Netherlands Embassy in Washington, D.C. He covered the cornucopias with hellebore leaves before filling them with Advocaat tulips. When you cluster tulips in a compact mass, he advises, "Put the full-blown flowers toward the center and the partially open ones around the edges."

Winter wanes in an arrangement by Birmingham's Louise Wrinkle. In a simple vase on a Chinese-style pedestal, she contrasts pale French tulips with still-bare branches of sweet gum. Mixing florist's offerings with cut boughs is an easy way to maximize impact.

Hyacinths have great natural appeal when massed in a potting soil-filled container, as Houston designer Herbert Wells does here. Don't worry with straightening stems. Let the flowers bow their heads, as they would in nature; the effect is one of a garden brought indoors.

N a t u r a l containers can bring new life to ordinary houseplants. Designer Stephen Black wraps a ficus tree's pot with florist's moss and places it in an antique wire basket. Valued any time of the year, a collection of French Palissy ware calls to mind an early garden.

M a g n i f y the effect of small flowers by displaying them in an extraordinary vase, as Candler Lloyd has done here with a three-tiered antique tole piece. You can justify what you splurge on the container by what you save on flowers you cut from your garden.

A l w a y s a classic: a few long stems in tall glass cylinders. In this case, the richly patterned panel of antique wallpaper is an ideal foil for the simple presentation by Amelia Handegan. To re-create the look, use an odd number of vases and stagger them along a table.

*S*UMMER

Nature over artifice reflects Nancy Braithwaite's style, whether she's designing a home or decorating for a special summer occasion. Braithwaite loves to "celebrate everything that is green and lovely about the country," and the tables she readies for guests follow suit. Visitors are greeted on the porch with favors of mint sprigs wrapped in handmade paper. Another unaffected welcome is extended by a centerpiece of white cosmos, heather, and Queen Anne's lace spilling from an apple basket.

Banners of breezy white voile instill a spirit of celebration from the moment guests arrive to attend a picnic reception in Mississippi. Designer Ellen Brown had a practical as well as an aesthetic purpose in mind when she fashioned these bridal standards. They mark the winding country lane leading to the lawn where the festivities will take place.

The porch is a perfect place for enjoying brunch in the cool morning air. Nancy Braithwaite likes to set her tables with a mix of classic and casual: Her best linens sparkle on burlap table skirts.

White linen is the quintessential fabric for summer entertaining. Braithwaite uses yards of it to dress her year-round outdoor furniture for a party. Beforehand, landscape artist Will Goodman paints a large-scale checkerboard pattern on the lawn. Outdoor striping paint—the kind used by landscapers—won't harm either the grass or guests' shoes.

Surprise friends and family by decorating tables with favorite things. Nancy and Dan Carithers did just that to make their wedding reception an affair to remember. To mark the bride's chair, they mounded baby's breath in a vintage backpack—picked up in the Adirondacks—and draped it over the back.

A cherub, an antique from seventeenth-century Italy, graces the bride's place setting, while an old shoe form found in Paris designates the groom's. Carithers jokes, "Ever since, we've called ourselves 'the angel and the old shoe.' "

Great style needn't be expensive. For these tablescapes, the bride and groom grew miniature boxwoods and topiaries of myrtle, rosemary, and thyme. Amid the greenery, they set bowls filled with white eggs and pitchers massed with cream-colored freesia and roses.

Garlands aren't only for Christmas, says Dorothy McDaniel, Birmingham floral designer. Her rose garland recalls the New Orleans tradition of crowning the bridal bed with a *ciel de lit,* or canopy. The garland would also make a memorable anniversary gift.

Whether a rope of flowers, such as French hydrangeas, or greenery spiced with a soupçon of blooms, summer garlands delight the soul. During the growing season, McDaniel suggests taking advantage of abundant flora to fashion an exuberant arrangement unmatched by a single bouquet. A garland's graceful lines can also enhance an entry or a dining room wall.

FALL

Sunflowers, cattails, wild grasses, and fennel all arrive blazing with the colors of autumn. When you use natural materials for indoor decorations, try for a grand scale to best represent the diversity and immensity of nature. "When we fill a vase with garden flowers and native grasses," says Birmingham floral designer Norman Kent Johnson, "we bring the substance of the season right into our home." This appealing arrangement has a secondary attraction: All of its materials can be conveniently found in your yard or in the woods, fields, or roadsides near your home.

D e t a i l s and imagination are essential to displays. A box resembling a picket fence embraces a miniature garden of coreopsis, Indian feather, and montebretia. "Even the finest shops," says Norman Kent Johnson, "cannot supply the wealth of offerings found in your garden."

Simplicity often means drama. Mary Douglas Drysdale selects amber sheaves of dried grasses to complement the colors in a portrait attributed to Sir Joshua Reynolds. The tones of the gilded frame, golden grasses, and dark wood come together for a vignette that glows.

S p r a y roses and plump rose hips add elegance to Norman Kent
Johnson's arrangement of nandina and holly. The large scale and
loosely spaced blooms give the impression of nonchalant grandeur.
F o r m a l table settings are warmed by casual floral decorations.
Amelia Handegan sets a small vase of statice at each setting and mounds
fruit and eucalyptus branches in a pair of compotes.

INTER

Whiter shades of pale are a recurring palette in the interiors of Washington, D.C., designer Frank Randolph. He therefore knows well that interesting textures are essential to neutral schemes. At Randolph's home, floral designer David Bell assembles miniature white pumpkins, dimpled winter squash, olive branches, and bay leaves. The stark mix of textures suggests the crispness of the winter landscape outdoors.

A closer look at his mantel arrangement of olive branches and bay leaves demonstrates Bell's knack for creating a festive look without disturbing the serenity of a neutral room. The mechanics couldn't be simpler, either: Among the branches he tucks a variety of limes, dried nuts, pinecones, and two white marble spheres.

For daughter Catherine's engagement party, Birmingham designer Ann Baker honors her heritage with a centerpiece of silver pitchers from three generations. Arranged with photos from family weddings, each pitcher is filled with a different creamy white flower.

White tulips seem to be a flower favored by many design-ers, and Richmond's Jane Molster is no exception. She appreciates their availability throughout winter and the fact that, even when used in a large centerpiece, they allow the china and gilded crystal to shine.

B i r c h   l o g s jostled together in a pine flat
prove that an effective seasonal display needn't contain
flowers. David Bell stands the limbs on end in a shal-
low box to complement the mottled stone fireplace in
a living room designed by Thomas Pheasant.

C a n   y o u think of a cozier dinner setting on a
winter's eve? Dan Carithers sets an inviting stage for an
intimate dinner for four, where firelight and candlelight
dance on splendid pieces of silver.

CHAPTER V

YOUR COLLECTIONS: Nothing in your home reveals more about you than these. They are fundamental to creating an environment that reflects something of yourself—your work and avocations, dreams and past experiences. Whether they're tortoiseshell boxes or books on Greek Revival architecture, your treasures are as distinguishing a feature as your signature. ● THE CHALLENGE comes in deciding how to display them. Collectibles, books, and artwork hold special meaning for us, and we naturally want to present them so that their significance is clear. Not only that, we want to arrange them in such a way that their aesthetic value is enhanced. How to do it? Here is where many of us can confess to feeling unsure. ● THE BEST APPROACH, in our experience, is to think of these displays

Your Own Stamp

as provocative vignettes. Such displays do more than simply showcase interesting objects; they combine single pieces in ways that command attention, suggest associations, and sharpen the senses. ● A CASE IN POINT is the setting on the facing page. Eating utensils made of horn, an on-going collection, are grouped to magnify their impact. Beautiful on its own merits, the still life also evokes a sense of the owners, Brian and Kathi Stringer of Houston, whose preoccupation with history and culture has been lifelong. ● SEEING HOW OTHERS have achieved this kind of individuality is the best way to learn how to do it yourself. Here are some of the most intriguing examples of collections we've seen, together with our observations on why we think they are displayed so effectively.

OLLECTIONS

L i n i n g the wall behind the bar with antique Persian tiles, Houston designer Herbert Wells skillfully incorporates his collection in his living room. Building or remodeling creates many opportunities for the permanent mounting of collections. Here, the vivid tiles brighten the neutral colors of the adjacent seating.

F i n i a l s salvaged from older buildings make a dramatic backdrop for a Venetian-style love seat. Rather than simply lining them up, Wells punctuates the graduation of heights with two or three smaller pieces. A miniature painting at the right end balances the composition. Though they've become expensive in recent years, these architectural-scale pieces have always been popular among designers and collectors.

Your Own Stamp

Small objects of similar shapes and materials characterize many a collection. But how do you make the repetition interesting? Memphis designers Steven Hickman and Tom Thomley illustrate one solution: a configuration based on contrast. Straight lines of boxes offset a pinwheel of antique seals, while the many diminutive pieces at the front of the table are anchored by more substantial ones at the back.

C o l o r can unify and amplify. Atlanta designer Carol Klotz subtly complements luminous ivory pieces with a mother-of-pearl card box and an English plate, while using a Chinese porcelain lamp for contrast. **A r r a n g i n g** containers in gridlike patterns emphasizes their uniformity and geometric appeal. For Brian Stringer, the technique works to organize his burled-walnut and tortoiseshell boxes. A basket of lemons freshens the table while maintaining the grid.

Porcelains from eighteenth-century China and cinnabar lacquered lunch baskets deserve pride of place commensurate with their quality. Dallas designer Beverly Field evokes a museum atmosphere with an orderly arrangement on shelves in this living room. The home gallery is considerably softened by an inviting seating group.

Flea-market porcelains make impressive groupings when colors harmonize. Jackye Lanham recommends arranging the plates on the floor first; then, when you've found a configuration that pleases your eye, hang the collection on the wall.

Vignettes may seem unstudied, but a closer look reveals much more. Birmingham designer Ellen Simonton uses lilac orchids to intensify the shadings of artisan David Bacharach's woven copper vessels. A round tray serves as an organizing back-drop for the woven vessels while directing attention to an early painting by Ida Kohlmeyer.

Original art can hold its own no matter what your deco-rating scheme. Here, a ceramic birdhouse by Debra Fritts and a new screen made from old prints are clearly at home with an exuberant mix of plum, cranberry, saffron, and chartreuse fabrics. This intense palette, by designer Carter Kay of Atlanta, belies the notion that artworks should be displayed only in gallery-white rooms.

H a n g   p a i n t i n g s close to the furniture below—a good rule is to separate them no more than ten inches. Ellen Simonton uses a series of objects, including a small painting by Toni Tully and a lamp by Winifred Ross, to link the tabletop to an Abtel encaustic.

Relating art to neighboring furniture engages the eye. The technique is admirably illustrated in the Florida home of Sam Ewing. Here, a large abstract painting by Jamali interacts with an English Regency table and modern pieces that are at once sculptural and neutral.

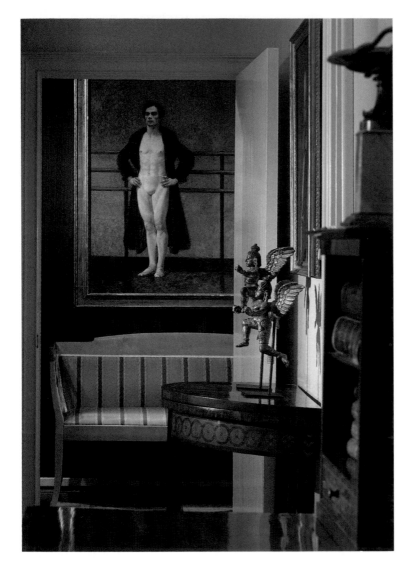

E m p h a s i s can be achieved through thoughtful placement. This portrait of Rudolf Nureyev by James Wyeth is displayed to stunning effect within a kind of second frame: the entry-hall doorway of Atlanta antiques dealers Arturo and Holly Melosi.

S i l h o u e t t e is the distinguishing feature of this delicate stoneware bowl by Richard DeVore, and it's displayed by art dealer Barbara Fendrick at a height that makes its outline apparent. Place a bowl with striking interior decoration on a low surface, such as a coffee table.

M i r r o r s can sometimes seem like large, uninspiring blocks. Houston designer Joe Shaffer advocates leaning interesting objects against them to break up the space and catch the eye. Over this fireplace, a Venetian mirror plays backup to a modern musical composition: an electric guitar that once belonged to Eric Clapton, a photograph of John Lennon, and lithographs from Lennon's "Bag One" suite.

Build dimension by leaning a small element against a larger one, as with this drawing and mirror. Also, consider what mirrors reflect. In Sam Ewing's bedroom, the reflection of an eighteenth-century bust creates an intriguing counterpoint to a figure drawing.

Dramatic lighting from recessed ceiling fixtures directs the eye toward prints by Willem de Kooning. Especially effective in a room of neutral colors, well-placed lighting creates highlights in this Atlanta living room designed by Charles Gandy and William Peace.

Diverse works become unified when displayed against a neutral fabric backdrop. To hang the pieces themselves, Washington, D.C., designer Jose Solis Betancourt used innovative fixtures mounted from the ceiling, allowing the fabric to fall freely behind the art.

*B*OOKS AND SHELVES

Fireside comforts, such as a volume or two from a trove of old books, are accentuated by a casual but sumptuous throw over the sofa. In this library of distinctively cultured allure, the books themselves summon the mood. An expansive collection fills floor-to-ceiling bookshelves original to this 1930s home in Washington, D.C. More volumes gather on tabletops and nestle beside the sofa, encouraging a sense of ease and accessibility. The yards-long portieres designed by Jose Solis Betancourt are both functional—to protect the shelves from dust—and decorative: The reversible fabric is toast-colored on one side for summer and brown on the other for winter. Ideas pulled from this grand example can work just as well in a more modest library. Placing a special book on a stand, for example, elicits interest and conversation.

Disarming disarray speaks volumes about this library's owner, Atlanta architect and designer Henri Jova. He forgoes conventional bookcases in favor of tables, chairs, and a desk. Stacks of books and mounds of magazines create the impression that reading is the owner's favorite pursuit.

Library tables of the eighteenth century provide precedent for designer Beverly Field. In showcasing her clients' favorite books, she varies the heights of the stacks and places decorative objects among them to make the display more interesting.

Harmonizing diverse objects in a space always involves some experimentation. To achieve the appealing look of well-filled shelves, begin by placing the largest volumes near the bottom, adjusting the shelf above to fit closely. Place smaller books on the middle and upper shelves, leaving open spaces for artwork and accessories. Add these objects last, and continue rearranging them until you strike a pleasing balance. Here, Herbert Wells worked with Picasso plates and Miró lithographs, but prized collectibles, folk art, or family photographs would also suffice.

Index

Contributors

Designers

Alexander Baer, 22–25, 74–75, 86, 87
Ann Baker, 114
Jim Barganier, 42
David Bell, 112, 117
Jose Solis Betancourt, 135, 136
Stephen Black, 31, 95
Nancy Braithwaite, 28, 48, 56, 57, 98, 100, 101
Gerrie Bremermann, 14–17
Ellen Brown, 98
Dan Carithers, 10–13, 54, 55, 65, 102, 103, 117
John Chrestia, 44
Stiles Colwill, 28, 68, 69
Duncan and Cris Connelly, 32
Joe Davis, 6, 42
Mary Douglas Drysdale, 18–21, 40, 67, 109
Patrick Dunne, 80
Sherry Durlach, 72
Sam Ewing, 129, 133
Francie Faudree, 38, 81
Jan Barboglio Feldman-Macdonald, 40
Barbara Fendrick, 130
Beverly Field, 124, 139
Charles Gandy, 134
Dale Gillman, 81
Kathy Guyton, 89
Amelia Handegan, 32, 44, 97, 110
Jane Hawkins Hoke, 79
Steven Hickman, 122
Brooke Huttig, 73
Norman Kent Johnson, 106, 108, 110
Henri Jova, 36, 138
Carter Kay, 126
Carol Klotz, 123
Jackye Lanham, 39, 79, 124
Candler Lloyd, 51, 96
Robert F. McAlpine, 46, 60, 70, 82
Dorothy McDaniel, 104–5
Joe McKinnon, 27
Mimi McMakin, 73
Arturo and Holly Melosi, 130
J. R. Miller, 78

Jane Molster, 115
William Peace, 134
Thomas Pheasant, 58–59, 77, 117
Frank Randolph, 112
Lyman Ratcliffe, 60
Gay Ratliff, 82
Mary Jane Ryburn, 91
Joe Shaffer, 132
Ellen Simonton, 126, 128
Cindy Smith, 50
Brian and Kathi Stringer, 84, 89, 119, 123
Tom Thomley, 122
Herbert Wells, 94, 120, 141
Vicente Wolf, 39
Marcel Wolterinck, 92
Louise Wrinkle, 92

Photographers

Ping Amranand, 58–59, 76–77
Antoine Bootz, 5 (center), 33, 40, 44, 90, 97, 123 (right)
Gary Clark, 105, back cover bottom right
Langdon Clay, 36–37, 38–39 (center), 51, 64–65, 79 (right), 96, 99, 111, 117 (right), 135, 136–37, 138
Cheryl S. Dalton, 32, 42, 72, 82–83, 102–3, 126
Dan Forer, 89 (right), 129, 133
Tina Freeman, 80
Mick Hales, 4 (top and center), 6, 8, 10 (top), 11, 18 (top), 19, 22–23, 24–25, 39 (right), 41, 43, 46–47, 61, 66–67, 70–71, 74–75, 78–79 (center), 86–87, 109, 116–17, 125, back cover top left, bottom left
Hickey-Robertson, 3, 5 (top and bottom), 12–13, 14–15, 16–17, 18 (bottom), 20–21, 30–31, 34–35, 38 (left), 45, 49, 50, 52, 54–55, 60, 62–63, 73, 78 (left), 81, 82 (left), 84–85, 88–89, 94–95, 115, 118, 120–21, 122–23 (center), 124,

130–31, 132, 138–39, 140–41, back cover top right
Jonathan Hillyer, 4 (bottom), 26, 98, 100–101, 122 (left), 127, 130
Chris A. Little, 134
Maxwell MacKenzie, 29, 68–69
Richard Moore, 10 (bottom)
Howard L. Puckett, 93, 104, 128
Angie Seckinger, 92, 112–13
John Vaughn, 28, 48, 56–57
Charles Walton IV, cover, 1, 106–7, 108, 110, 114, jacket flap

Contributing Editors

Carol Isaak Barden
Caroline B. Campbell
David Dillon
Susan Stiles Dowell
Marion Fox
Palmer Graham
Lisa Ruffin Harrison
Emyl Jenkins
Marjorie H. Johnston
Virginia D. Moseley
Shelby Neely
Susan Ripley-Hilliard
Mary Jane Ryburn
Liz Seymour
Sallie Beckwith Smith
Prudence Squier
John Villani
Lucy Woodson

Special Thanks

Ainsworth-Noah, Atlanta
Birmingham Museum of Art
Jill E. Hasty
Dina N. Moorer
Christina Wynn